D0314903

HIGH CARD FLUSH:
A POCKET GUIDE

HIGH CARD FLUSH:
A POCKET GUIDE

Michael Wehking

Copyright © 2018 by Michael Wehking.

Library of Congress Control Number:		2018904234
ISBN:	Hardcover	978-1-9845-2071-5
	Softcover	978-1-9845-2070-8
	eBook	978-1-9845-2069-2

All rights reserved. No part of this book may be reproduced or transmitted
in any form or by any means, electronic or mechanical, including photocopying,
recording, or by any information storage and retrieval system,
without permission in writing from the copyright owner.

Any people depicted in stock imagery provided by Getty Images are models,
and such images are being used for illustrative purposes only.
Certain stock imagery © Getty Images.

Print information available on the last page.

Rev. date: 04/10/2018

To order additional copies of this book, contact:
Xlibris
1-888-795-4274
www.Xlibris.com
Orders@Xlibris.com
777766

CONTENTS

Introduction

High Card Flush!

Nicknamed Flush, it's not the middle-aged female facial blush that goes with menopause. But this poker game can make your face red in either elation or anger. It's the rollercoaster of poker games.

Like my book: Winning Three Card Poker, Flush is a casino table game that pays out some big-time jackpots. Winners get paid for getting flushes that range from three to seven cards. The true big-time payouts are the straight Flush variety. This dandy jackpot was delivered by Jana the other day.

I've won some mega jackpots playing Flush. In fact, the first hand I was ever dealt was 7-8-9-10-J of Clubs on a three-way $25 bet. Get out the calculator… that's 2- to 1 on pairs plus 100 to 1 on straight Flush plus winning the ante and bet! That Jackpot exceeded $2500!

The game is great and sports lots of action! It's one of the most popular games at Harrahs and the tables dealing it are

usually full! It's only been around since 2011 and you'll find a nice pack of ladies at every table.

A big key to playiing is smart betting! You need to double your ante from what you bet on your pairs plus and straight flush bets. For me, I bet $25 on the front two circles and $75 on back. After looking at your cards, you should stay on any three card flush higher than Q-10-2. You'll win your ante and bet 60 percent of the time. You'll see gigantic payouts but also suffer long droughts. Key is patience and a large bank roll. Isn't that the key to all table games?

Start with $300 as I advocate doing that in most games and bet 1 red on each for forward circle and three red on the ante. That way you'll get at least $5 on all winning hands unless you get a four-card flush or three-card straight flush or better!

CHAPTER 1

If you've read my first book, you know the deal! Bigger bets gelt bigger payouts! Make sure your pit boss logs you in, tip well, sit back, show confidence and be mighty humble. This game brings patience to a whole new level.

You'll go a couple hands with epic payouts then you hit long dry spells, hence the bankroll requirement. Here's some fun action from Harrah's in Tahoe in the early morning wee hours!

A super nice hand brought to you by Mo from Iran. He enjoyed my tips which filled his files, these little plastic cylinders, to the rims. Even tossed $25 at my waitress. Yes, tip well and know that your key assistants want you to win big. Harrah's offers free booze in Tahoe, one of the most beautiful places I've seen on earth!

Let's talk bank roll and getting money for nothing now. If you're a true gambler, you'll want a credit line established at your playgrounds. It's called a marker. All big-time players use them. It quashes the need to go to the cashier and rack up mega surcharges for cash that exceed $70 per thousand at Harrahs in Tahoe.

If you feel you mastered three card poker and high card Flush tables, saunter into high stakes and plop down on a good draw poker machine. its 425 a hand and hold on tight. Make sure you choose game with a progressive jackpot, have a full drink and an empty bladder.

These games make you lose all track of time and boast a 20 percent house advantage, making them prohibitive for daily wagering. Racked up up another W2G with this jackpot! Had a lot of fun, crushed my tier points and ballooned my reward credits on this before the big 'boom' struck. They always surprise you and send a happy shiver down your spine when the 'call attendant' notification aooears as this one did!

Make sure you get outside, eat something and visit your local casino host. They can provide you with a wealth of information about local hot spots, specials and Diamond Club hours. My wife loves The Diamond Club. It's a great refueling station and a place off the beaten path where you'll unwind, rehydrate, grab a bite and count your winnings. Also a great place to catch up on news, and make a plan for your next, big score.

You'll need a card to enter as these places are coveted much like the Secen Star card. Slide it in the slot and enter nirvana. Tahoe sports a great, clean club with all the perks and a friendly Army of staff to serve you.

This card is so golden it gets you comped suites, limo tides to and from airport, nice dinners, free cashier advances and even ocean cruises, free drinks and food an an annual trip free. Can't beat that!

CHAPTER 2

Losing

About the time you think it's all under control and you're invincible, defeat rears it's ugly head. I experienced this at Harrahs Tahoe on a Friday, getting smoked for $4100 while playing three card poker and high card Flush.

I would get up $1300-$2000 only to be beaten back down. I quit, grabbed some sleep and recharged for a grand Saturday. That day started at 3 am with a win on five card draw poker slot for a W2G payout of $2000 followed by a mimosa-induced Royal Flush that netted $8480 and I grabbed the photo to prove it!

The morale of the story? Resilience! When you get beat, take it like a man, retreat, cleanup, recharge and come out confident because our winning betting formulas will get the job done. I treated myself to a new watch, passing on the TAG Huer $4400 model and the cashier tossed in a black set of Ray Ban shades. Momentous from an epic weekend! This was all before 11 am.

Gaming is fun, productive and the posse following me around the casino got quite large after I hit the Royal Flush. A trip outside to clear my head with a burrito breakfast at Hard Rock got back on task.

CHAPTER 3

Helping others

I make it a point to advise the uninformed. When they learn I wrote. Winning Three Card Poker and start to readjust, they're chip stacks grow. I politely ask them to pass it on.

As I wrote in my last book, I am amazed at how many people have no clue how to bet. They toss nickels on the circles and when they win, they push. That's just wrong and it'll derail your gambling ambitions and leave you cash short in some pretty neat locales.

There were people who taught me how to bet and I vowed I'd never be dressy at the table. That goes for tipping! Pay it forward to your dealers and cashier staff. They rely on tips to make house and car payments and send their kids to college. I

tipped the bartender who made that tasty mimosa 4100. And I also tipped the attendant who paid me a cool $8000 when I won.

I make it a point to try and fill dealer vials with red chips. The cashiers have a stressful job and deserve your generosity as well. it all goes toward boosting the local economy and it's the right thing to do!

So its time for a mid-day break. Go yo your room, place your fortune in the safe and lock it up! Grab a nap, some water and get your mind off poker so you can be ready to shine at night.

Chapter 4

A family Affair

Be a leader. As the family patriarch, it's my duty to train the wife and kids in the finer art of gaming. Give tools, fill up their bamk rolls and unleash em. Like a lion in the jungle who tears apart a hyena so his brood can feed, you must lay the fruits of gaming at your collective family's feet.

Before you do all this, make them read about losing. And like any goo Army operations pla, ensure they understand the mission, it's rewards and the major stumbling blocks,

If the family is sharp, they'll make bank, help others and payoff all debt, leaving a lasting legacy.

Don't be the poor parent who loses, spending their priceless inheritance carelessly. Kids wanna be like their parents. Pass on

your tips, values and class. It's a gift that should keep on giving. So darn proud of my kids, their work ethics and all they've done. They've stayed on track through tough times. I will take some credit for that.

The best thing you can do for your family is teach, provide and evaluate. Don't let them develop poor habits like smoking, heavy drinking or treating people poorly. Your family reflects you and their behaviors are on display and will be constant scrutiny

Start a 501C3 for grand kids early and pile in lots money. College will be super speedy in 18 years.

CHAPTER 5

Documenting Success

I've told you about all perks, now you need to get organized. Save every receipt, keep track of winnings and ensure you deposit and withdraw monies from a major bank via credit and debit cards. This part is critical to the health of your financial fortune,

Get a good, attorney, start a limited liability company 9llc0 and prepare to take off. Travel, meals, clothing, vehicles and incidentals are huge expenses. A typical tripfour-day in Vegas could run you thousands.

Create a tabbed three-ringed binder to track all aspects of your company and it'll pay huge dividends.

Then create an irrevocable trust and appoint a qualified trustee to manage, invest your fortune. Too many spend less time financial than they would on a morning run. If you're a millionaire, act, plan and invest like one.

With all your notoriety you're gonna attract attention which draws trap hangers. These are folks too last to grind at casinos. They want handouts and they'll concoct any of story to try to get themselves on your payroll.

Which brings you to your employees. If you made it, you'll need a staff, complete with a concierge, maid, accountant and lawyer. Oversight of them is critical. Mice eat when the cats asleep. Know your net worth and conduct monthly meetings to oversee your financial juggxrnaught.

Finally, I'll talk about health. Gaming may seem lucrative and easy but it has a lot of hidden threats. Smoking fills the table areas. Then couple poor eating, potential sleeplessness and a myriad of other issues that could plague you. Get an annual physical, get exercise, drink a lot of water and grab engage in some healthy hobbies outside the casino.

Don't be afraid to take a well-deserved vacation, a guys-only fishing weekend, or a bucket-list golf outing. I'm headed to

the April 2018 masters to recharge, golf and spend time with friends. Time away from the casino with positive people and productive outlets will keep you sharp and very happy.

Finally, you're going to have a lot of money to park. Invest in an escape second home. Plan and goon great vacations. You've earned it. Ensure you're family is able to enjoy the fruits of your labor and by all means have a lot of insurance. As the bread winner, your accountant needs to set you up with great life, health and long-term care policies.

Now that you've made it, splurge on the super bowl tickets, the Armani suit, the country club membership and the car of your dreams. You have earned it, be the light, Stay humble, keep God in your life, and I'll meet you in The Diamond Club.

CHAPTER 6

'Flushing' and Getting 'Flushed'

I experienced both sides of the coin on my recent trip to Harashs, Tahoe. That is, I won big and lost big on High Card Flush in a 24-hour stretch. The win exceeded $2200 on a run from about 3-5 am. I pretty much max bet the circles and at this casino max bet is $200 per circle except for Flush circle. That's laying out $700 a pop.

I won hitting three-card straight flushes that paid seven times the bet or $1400 per win. I hit three of those during that stretch, getting up about 43100 at one time. I left the table for coffee and a donut up $2400 and tipped the dealer probably 75 bucks during my play.

Conversely, I also got flushed despite being a professional gambler. I sat at the table with Julie, a middle-aged blond who drank Fuji, fidgeted with her cards and could've passed for being the captain of her high school dance line. She was hot,

And smart. At least she played smart. She was a nickel better who spent the day at the table at first base.

I mention her because you'll meet new friends and build a lot of relationships gaming. Julie is married and loves Flush.

I started out winning big as I had brought $2000 to the table after a successful winning three card poker stint. I won a couple three card straight hands and even won a couple 9-high three card Flush hands. I got a little cavalier which is never good.

The dealer took me out on with a five card heart flush versus my solid four card Ace-high Club Flush. As my third $700-dollar loss in a row, I excited the table smartly, losing $1900. I took the remaining hundred to video poker and parlayed it to this little gem. The casino offers banks of video poker games tied to a progressive jackpot which in this case was $4400.

I just finished Michael Wehking's High Card Flush! Great read.

In fact, HCF! is a *must read* if 1) you enjoyed his first release (Winning 3-Card Poker), 2) are a *wannabe* professional gambler, or 3) just want to learn what makes this author tick.

HCF! works because the author does such a solid job of walking his talk. Example. He calls out humility as an essential gambler's core value. Wehking takes the next step, too, and models the value by sharing concrete examples of cases in which his own lack of humility cost him real money. That highlights another reason both books worked for me: Wehking's authenticity. It's clear the author wants his readers to be as successful as he's been, but it's just as clear that he's not going to romanticize his experiences or his success. He keeps it real.

The images in HCF! add to its authenticity. Readers actually *see* the author at the table, see hiswinning hands, see his dealers, see his family, and, most importantly, see that he's describing his experiences, not just his theories.

That balance between the theoretical and the practical shows itself best in Weking's approach to gambling as a profession rather than a hobby. He not only advises his readers about how to make money but how to keep it, and, as is his style, he gives readers the tools they need to follow his advice. Creating a corporation, meticulously tracking expenses, hiring a good lawyer, and regularly evaluating your employee's performances aren't the typical guides-to-successful-gambling, but after reading HCF! readers wouldn't consider a careen in high stakes gambling without having those tools in their belts.

— Harry McLenighan, Ed.D.